One, Two, Three, Oops!

For all at Holy Family School,
Southampton
M.C.

For Carrie Rose
G.W.

MAGI PUBLICATIONS
1 The Coda Centre, 189 Munster Road,
London SW6 6AW
www.littletigerpress.com
First published in Great Britain 1998

Printed in Belgium

ISBN 1 85430 471 2

One, Two, Three, Oops!

by Michael Coleman
illustrated by Gwyneth Williamson

MAGI PUBLICATIONS

Mr and Mrs Rabbit had a big family . . .

A *very* big family . . .

A very, *very* big family!

"I wonder how many babies we've got?"
said Mr Rabbit one morning. "I think I'll
count them."

"Why not wait until later?" said Mrs Rabbit.
"I would."

"No," said Mr Rabbit firmly. "I'll do it now."

So outside he went to where the babies were playing. Mr Rabbit started counting.

"One, two, three – oops! Oh, noggin-sploggin!" he exclaimed.

With a hop and a skip, the babies he'd
counted ran off to join their brothers
and sisters. He couldn't tell which ones
he'd counted and which he hadn't.

Mr Rabbit started again. This time he got a little further. "One, two, three, four – oops! Oh, noggin-sploggin, boodle-doodle!" he grumbled.

The babies had started a game of tag
and moved. He'd lost count again.

Mr Rabbit tried one more time.
"One, two, three, four, five – oops!
Oh, noggin-sploggin, boodle-doodle,
grizzly-wizzly!" he groaned.

The babies had started playing hide and seek.
Now he couldn't see any of them. He'd lost
count again.

"This is no good," said Mr Rabbit. "I'll have
to think of a better way."

So he sat and thought – until he had a good idea. "I know," he said. "I'll give a carrot to every baby I count. That way I'll see the ones I've missed."

So Mr Rabbit started counting again. This time he gave a carrot to each baby he counted. "One, two, three, four, five, six – oops! Oh, noggin-sploggin, boodle-doodle, grizzly-wizzly, sniffy-whiffy!" he cried.

The babies he'd
given carrots to
had eaten them!
He couldn't tell
who he'd counted
and who he hadn't.

"I know," said Mr Rabbit,
as he had another good idea.
"I'll tell them to sit down
when I've counted them.
That way I won't get
mixed up."

So Mr Rabbit told his babies to sit down once he'd counted them. "One, two, three, four, five, six, seven – oops! Oh, noggin-sploggin, boodle-doodle, grizzly-wizzly, sniffy-whiffy, jingle-bingle!" he shouted.

The ground was full of prickly weeds. Just as soon
as a baby sat down, it jumped up again! Mr Rabbit
had lost count once more!

"Right, this will *definitely* work," said Mr Rabbit,
as he had yet another idea. "I'll send every baby
indoors. The ones still outside will be the ones
I haven't counted. I can't possibly get muddled
up that way!"

So Mr Rabbit started counting again. This time, every baby he counted was sent indoors.

"One, two, three, four, five, six, seven, eight – oops! Oh, noggin-sploggin, boodle-doodle, grizzly-wizzly, sniffy-whiffy, jingle-bingle, fuddle-duddle!" yelled Mr Rabbit, stamping his foot.

He'd forgotten that their home had
a back door. Every baby he'd sent in
the front had run straight out the back.
He'd lost count yet again.

Mr Rabbit sat down and thought once more. He thought all afternoon . . .

. . . and he thought all evening. And then he noticed a patch of mud on the ground and had his best idea yet.

"I've got it!" said Mr Rabbit. "Every time
I count a baby I'll put mud on its tail.
Then I'll know that the babies with clean
tails are the ones I haven't counted. I can't
possibly get muddled that way."

So Mr Rabbit began to count once more.
Every time he counted a baby, he put a
blob of mud on its tail. "One, two, three,
four, five, six, seven, eight, nine – oops!
Oh, noggin-sploggin, boodle-doodle,
grizzly-wizzly, sniffy-whiffy, jingle-bingle,
fuddle-duddle, jungle-bungle!"
he roared, jumping up
and down . . .

It had started to rain. All the blobs of mud he'd put on the babies he'd counted had been washed off. He'd lost count yet again!

"I give up!" said Mr Rabbit. He stomped angrily back indoors. "I don't know how to count those babies!" he cried. "I'm fed up!"

At that moment Mr and Mrs Rabbit's babies scampered back indoors. Tired and happy after playing all day they were soon fast asleep.

"I told you to wait till later," said Mrs Rabbit. "Now try counting them."

Mr Rabbit began counting once again.
"One, two, three, four, five, six, seven,
eight, nine, TEN!" he cried. "I've done it!"
"Oh no you haven't," said Mrs Rabbit . . .

"You've forgotten the littlest ones!"